# The Labyrinth:
## A Spiritual Journey

**Ancient Myth**
modern meaning

# The Labyrinth: A Spiritual Journey

Ellyn Sanna with Kenneth McIntosh

ANAMCHARA BOOKS

# The Labyrinth: A Spiritual Journey

*Ellyn Sanna with Kenneth McIntosh*

Copyright © 2012 by Anamchara Books,
a Division of Harding House Publishing Service, Inc.
All rights reserved. No part of this publication may be reproduced or transmitted in any form or by any means, electronic or mechanical, including photocopying, recording, taping, or any information storage and retrieval system, without permission from the publisher.

Anamchara Books
220 Front Street
Vestal, NY 13850

First Printing

9 8 7 6 5 4 3 2 1

ISBN: 978-1-933630-87-8

Library of Congress Control Number 2011910805

Cover design by Ellyn Sanna.
Interior design by Camden Flath.
Printed in the United States of America.

# Contents

Introduction: What Is a Labyrinth?   7
I. The Classical Labyrinth: The Hidden Monster   25
II. The Pagan Labyrinth: The Goddess at the Center   47
III. The Medieval Labyrinth: The Christian Pilgrimage   69
IV. The Modern Labyrinth: A Threefold Journey   85

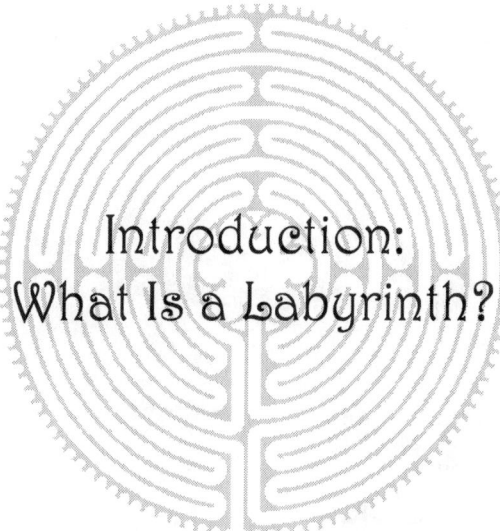

# Introduction: What Is a Labyrinth?

Then it seemed like falling into a labyrinth:

we thought we were at the finish,

but our way bent round

and we found ourselves as it were

back at the beginning,

and just as far from

that which we were seeking at first.

—Socrates

## Introduction: What is a Labyrinth?

The labyrinth is one of the most ancient of human visual symbols. It is an image that has haunted the human imagination for thousands of years, since the first human beings drew the earliest spiral patterns and told their earliest myths. For earlier, simpler cultures, each detail of nature had meaning. To repeat the intricate curved shapes of seashells and spider webs, coiling snakes and vine tendrils, the slick curls of intestines or the far-flung shining spiral of the Milky Way, was to call forth that meaning. It was more than just an interesting pattern; it *meant* something.

> These labyrinthine spirals
> indicate the symbolic passageway
> from the visible realm of the human
> into the invisible dimension of the divine.
> —Ami Ronnberg

The ancient Mesoamericans, for example, created the spiral pattern of snail shells over and over in their artwork. Like a labyrinth, the snail shell curves inward, a tunnel that leads through enclosing walls to a secret heart at the center. The early Aztecs, Nahuatl, and Maya connected the snail shell to female sexuality, to birth and death. "To perish is to be born," they wrote in their chronicles, and the coil of the snail's shell became for them a powerful symbol of resurrection.

> Like the snail that builds its own slow house,
> we too create the coiling pathway of our lives,
> a secret labyrinth within our hearts
> that leads us slowly, surely
> toward the moment
> when we die—
> and are born again.
> —Evelyn Harris

# Introduction: What is a Labyrinth?

# The Labyrinth: A Spiritual Journey

The spider web, another natural labyrinth, has been connected in various myths to the mystery of creation (since a spider creates her web with material from her own body). For Carl Jung, the spider web was a symbol of wholeness, pointing toward the intricate unity of the universe. Western culture came to associate spider webs with witches and death, but African and Native American cultures saw the spider and her labyrinthine structure as symbols of wisdom and feminine creativity. (Westerners have had an unfortunate but deep-seated tendency to connect feminine symbols with evil and darkness!)

I dreamed I was tiny.

And I was crawling around and around a spider web.

When I reached the center,

I found something wonderful.

I wish I could remember what it was.

—Ashley, age seven

# The Labyrinth: A Spiritual Journey

> If you are facing in the right direction,
> all you need to do is keep on walking.
> — Buddhist saying

The labyrinth's spiral shape was never intended to be the same as a maze. A maze is a mental puzzle, with false passageways and dead ends—but a labyrinth has only a single path; there is no chance you will go astray, so long as you follow the path. Like a snail's shell, the single opening leads to the center, without any intersection to offer the possibility of choice, and then the passage returns to the outside, all the while moving back and forth in the most circuitous way possible so as to completely fill the interior space. A labyrinth is more than simply an interesting visual pattern or architectural construction, more than the maze's game. Humans have always seen in the labyrinth a symbol of life's deepest meanings.

# Introduction: What is a Labyrinth?

Thus the present-day notion of a labyrinth

as a place where one can lose one's way

must be set aside.

It is a confusing path,

hard to follow without a thread,

but, provided [the traveler]

is not devoured at the midpoint,

it leads surely,

despite twists and turns,

back to the beginning.

—Carl Kerényi

> If life's journey be endless
> where is its goal?
> The answer is, it is everywhere.
> We are in a palace which has no end,
> but which we have reached.
> By exploring it
> and extending our relationship with it
> we are ever making it
> more and more our own.
> —Rabindranath Tagore

## Introduction: What is a Labyrinth?

The labyrinth may seem like a simple construction, but for the person who enters it, there is no sense of going anywhere. The destination is unseen; both the way in and the way out seem impossible. The path takes the journeyer past the destination again and again. There is no choice but to go on, but without the benefit of a bird's-eye view, it can seem a hopeless journey.

> To travel hopefully is a better thing than to arrive,
> and the true success is to labor.
> — Robert Louis Stevenson

> How often I found where I should be going
> only by setting out for somewhere else.
> —Buckminster Fuller

At its most basic level, the labyrinth confuses us. It forces us to abandon our preference for straight lines; linear thinking will get us nowhere when we are within the labyrinth's walls. It insists that we let go of our own sense of direction, our demands for measureable goals, our need to move from point A to point B by the shortest, most efficient route possible.

# Introduction: What is a Labyrinth?

From within,

the view is extremely restricted and confusing,

while from above,

one discovers a supreme artistry and order.

Thus the labyrinth simultaneously

incorporates confusion and clarity,

multiplicity and unity,

imprisonment and liberation,

chaos and order.

—Penelope Reed Doob

# The Labyrinth: A Spiritual Journey

The labyrinth is not efficient! It requires that we abandon ~~rational~~ thought, that we consent to be lost. Ancient cultures used the labyrinth as part of initiation rites for this very reason: because when our consciousness is temporarily confused, when we are forced to let go of what we think we know, new truth can be revealed to us.

Anthropologists have said that the labyrinth is the Western world's version of the Eastern mandala, the sacred circle used to both symbolize and embody the unity of the universe. Both are more than diagrams, more than pleasing visual patterns; both lead us to consider the meaning of our lives in new ways.

> Do not fear going forward slowly.
>
> Fear only to stand still.
>
> — Chinese proverb

Introduction: What is a Labyrinth?

# The Labyrinth: A Spiritual Journey

## Introduction: What is a Labyrinth?

> The soul walks not upon a line,
>
> neither does it grow like a reed.
>
> The soul unfolds itself,
>
> like a lotus of countless petals.
>
> — Kahlil Gibran

# I
# The Classical Labyrinth: The Hidden Monster

We each have a part of our nature that we have a rejected,

a monstrous, twisted creature,

the illegitimate child

who proves we've been unfaithful:

a Minotaur.

We hide this beast deep inside us,

where no one will ever catch a glimpse of it,

not even (especially) ourselves.

And yet, echoing from the labyrinthine

depths of our own hearts,

we hear the beast's roars of pain.

The thunder of its angry hooves shakes our being.

—Judith Nystrom Kennedy

## The Classical Labyrinth: The Hidden Monster

King Minos had a terrible secret, one he sought to hide from the world. His wife, Pasiphae, had fallen in love with a huge white bull. That alone would have been shameful enough, but Pasiphae had conceived a child from her illicit affair, a horrifying monster that was part human and part bull. Minos could not bear to see the proof of his wife's adultery, and so he built a labyrinth—and he hid the Minotaur, the hideous, rejected child, at the very center.

> It is the Minotaur
> who conclusively justifies the existence of the Labyrinth.
> —Jorge Luis Borges

The entire myth's cast lives within you.

The jealous King Minos is you.

The infatuated and heartbroken Queen Pasiphae is you.

And most of all the Minotaur is you.

You have betrayed yourself.

You have hidden your deepest shame

inside the labyrinth of your heart.

And you will never know peace

until you go in and confront it.

—Jayne Silverberry

## The Classical Labyrinth: The Hidden Monster

But although the Minotaur was hidden away from sight, King Minos could not forget him—nor was the Minotaur easy to forget, since deep in the dark of night, his bellows of rage and hunger echoed through the palace. Consumed with shame and frustration, the king lashed out at his enemies, the Athenians, demanding they sacrifice to the Minotaur seven young men and seven young women every ninth year.

What do you sacrifice to the monster that lives inside you?

The people you encounter?

The people you love?

Yourself?

— Judith Nystrom Kennedy

> A labyrinthine man never seeks the truth,
> but only his Ariadne.
> —Friedrich Nietzsche

The terrible feast continued every nine years—until on the third cycle of nine years, Theseus was one of the young men who came to Crete to be sacrificed to the Minotaur. Theseus was determined to kill the monster rather than be killed by it, and the king's daughter, Ariadne, fell in love with the brave young man.

Ariadne gave Theseus a sword and the end of a thread from her spool, so he would not become confused within the labyrinth and would be able to find his way out again. Theseus fought the Minotaur, killed him, and emerged triumphant from the labyrinth.

We want to be in control.
We want to map our own life.
Ultimately, life almost always requires
that we simply surrender control,
and trust the direction that comes to us
from something outside,
our Ariadne's thread.
It could be a relationship.
It could be a job,
or parenthood.
Always, it is something
we cannot control
that leads us on a path
we could never have predicted.
—Annie Brown

# The Labyrinth: A Spiritual Journey

Ariadne's thread was known as a "clew," the root meaning of our modern word "clue": something that points the way, something seemingly small that helps us unwind a greater meaning. Feminist scholars have viewed the thread's role in the labyrinth story as a connection to women as spinners and weavers, to the Fates (the three women who spun the thread of human life), and to still more ancient feminine symbols of spider and web.

> The great awareness comes slowly, piece by piece.
> The path of spiritual growth is a path of lifelong learning.
> —M. Scott Peck

The Ego, the monster, wants what it wants.

It is hungry, always hungry,

and it will consume everything in its path

in its futile attempt to sate his hunger.

Theseus is the Everyman Hero who comes to kill the Monster,

to stop the endless sacrifice.

But he cannot succeed without giving in to Ariadne—

and following her lead.

Ariadne, the embodiment of emptiness

and the transcendence of Ego,

the utterly passive and submissive,

is the only one who can lead Theseus

through the complex labyrinth and back out again.

His... ego is no better than the Minotaur he seeks to slay—

his ego, is in fact, the Minotaur itself.

Only by this submission to Ariadne,

in seeking her help, can he succeed.

—Adam Zatheos

Life may seem inexplicable.

But always, somewhere,

there is a narrow filament of meaning,

like a spider web.

Hold it between the thumb and finger or your heart.

Follow its invisible trail through the labyrinth of your life,

until it leads you where it will.

This is the walk of faith,

this blind stepping in the darkness,

with only the invisible, resilient wisp of thread

that leads to God.

—Gerda Crake

## The Classical Labyrinth: The Hidden Monster

The human child has left its mother's womb,

the center of the labyrinth,

and begun its voyage ...

a process of unwinding, unwinding

of the umbilical cord,

which is nothing other than the thread of Ariadne,

as inalienable a part of the Labyrinth

as the Minotaur.

—Helmut Jaskolksi

> Get to know the monster that lives in your own soul,
>
> dive deep into your soul and explore it.
>
> —Tori Amos

In the classical stories, the monster is an essential aspect of the labyrinth. The hero only ventures inside the labyrinth to find and defeat that terrible beast. And yet the monster is no alien creature. Like Luke Skywalker in *Star Wars*, eventually each hero realizes the enemy is related to him by blood. That is life's most terrible, most intimate, and most shameful secret. The monster is not "out there"—it is buried deep inside us, bone of our bone and flesh of our flesh.

## The Classical Labyrinth: The Hidden Monster

The Minotaur is a metaphor for the mirror
you do not wish to look into.
It is the portrait of Dorian Grey,
the man under Darth Vader's mask,
the skeleton in your closet.
Half-man and half-bull,
it is all of your humanity and all of your animal tendencies
wrapped up into one—then buried in a dark hole to fester.
It is all that you wish to deny you are.

—Samantha L. Noto

But at the same time, the Minotaur's name in the ancient story is also Asterion, which means "the starry one." The terribly deformed creature that lives within the labyrinth is also connected to light and stars, to a celestial vision. The thing we most fear, our most shameful secret, is also, somehow, the thing that will ultimately lead us to God.

> What we call monsters can be experienced as sublime.
>
> They represent powers too vast
>
> for the normal forms of life to contain them.
>
> —Joseph Campbell

## The Classical Labyrinth: The Hidden Monster

You cannot escape the monster.

You must face it.

There is no way to reach the labyrinth's center,

the perfect point,

except by looking the monster in the face—

and there you will see both yourself

and God.

—Jayne Silverberry

By a monster I mean some horrendous presence or apparition
that explodes all of your standards for
harmony, order, and ethical conduct.
—Joseph Campbell

Let your mind start a journey through a strange new world.
Leave all thoughts of the world you knew before.
. . . and you'll live as you've never lived before.
—Erich Fromm

# The Classical Labyrinth: The Hidden Monster

> We have only to follow the thread
>
> of the hero path.
>
> And where we thought
>
> to find an abomination,
>
> we shall find God.
>
> And where we thought to slay another,
>
> we shall slay ourselves.
>
> —Joseph Campbell

Ultimately, we must be willing to love the monster, so that the monster can be transformed. We must kill that selfish, hidden aspect at our deepest, darkest core—and at the same time we must take it into ourselves. When the monster is no longer rejected and abandoned, it can be changed.

And then it becomes to us the messenger of God, the very thing we needed to crash through all the walls we had built to keep the Divine outside our lives.

> The beast residing at the center of the labyrinth
> is also an angel.
> —Thomas Moore

## The Classical Labyrinth: The Hidden Monster

# II
# The Pagan Labyrinth: The Goddess at the Center

Labyrinths were the sites for sacred springtime ceremonies in the ancient pagan communities of the Celts and other groups across Europe. A young woman would play the part of the mother goddess and take her place at the center of the labyrinth, which symbolized the netherworld. Then a man playing the role of the sky god would free the goddess from her captivity and restore her to the world above, where he would marry her, symbolizing the return of the Earth's fertility. This reenactment of the ancient story (better known to us today through the lens of the classical tale of Persephone) was a central part of pagan spirituality, an affirmation of the eternal promise of new life.

> No winter lasts forever;
> no spring skips its turn.
> —Hal Borland

## The Pagan Labyrinth: The Goddess at the Center

The oldest pagan labyrinths were feminine symbols. The Roman Christian world feared this ancient view of the spiritual realm; it saw the Goddess as a witch who threatened the eternal salvation of men's souls. The Christian God was sternly masculine, unable to encompass within the Divine Person the qualities of both father and mother, male and female. But for pagan believers, the labyrinth's Goddess was a call to faith in the power and promise of Divine love.

> The Goddess, the Mother,
> the turning spiral that whirls us in and out of existence,
> whose winking eye is the pulse of being—
> birth, death, rebirth.
>
> —Miriam Simos

When the hero wound his way through the labyrinth, it was a voyage toward hope, a journey to resurrection, both for the hero and for the community as a whole. The hero's success meant the entire world would be reborn to new life; his fulfillment brought promise to everyone.

We are accustomed to think of the spiritual journey as a very private affair. The ancient pagans and aboriginal people around the world have always looked at things quite differently. The community cannot survive without the individual quest. When the hero rescues the girl at the center of the labyrinth, the entire world is remade—and the entire world celebrates. The fulfillment of the individual, the human community, and the planet itself are inextricably braided together.

> The good we secure for ourselves is precarious and uncertain
> until it is secured for all of us and incorporated into our common life.
>
> —Jane Addams

## The Pagan Labyrinth: The Goddess at the Center

For the strong desire of every living thing
is waiting for the revelation of the children of God.
For every living thing was put under the power of change,
not by its desire, but by the One who made it so, in hope
that all living things will be made free from the power of death
and will have a part with the free children of God in glory.

—Romans 8:19–22

Scholars of the ancient world tell us that at the oldest levels of human history, the labyrinth has always been connected to the holy feminine. If that's the case, the Greeks may have completely misinterpreted the story of Crete's labyrinth, casting villains as heroes, and heroes as villains. Instead, the story may have gone like this: In order for new life to be born each year, the bull-man, the embodiment of masculine fertility, had to carry out a sacred marriage in the center of the labyrinth, the dark cave-womb of the goddess. This return to the womb was both dangerous and life-giving. The king—the bull-man—had to die first, in order that new life could spring from his blood.

> If a seed of grain does not go into the earth and come to an end,
> it is still a seed and no more;
> but through its death it gives much fruit.
> —Jesus (John 12:24)

Whether or not the Greeks twisted the original meaning of the labyrinth story, the essential meanings are not so very different, and even misunderstandings can prove fruitful and creative. In the end, it makes little difference if we confront the monster at the center of the labyrinth—or the goddess who both weds and kills, sacrifices and gives birth to new life. Either way, this twisting journey is terrifying, perilous, and ultimately, triumphant.

A person cannot be resurrected until he dies; rebirth requires that we first let go of all we once were so we can become something new. Each year dies in the cold of winter—and the new spring that follows is both the same and utterly new. This same cycle of death and rebirth is the ancient heart of both Christianity and paganism.

> Christ has died.
> 
> Christ is risen.
> 
> Christ will come again.
> 
> —The Mystery of Faith, the Roman Missal

"The journey of the labyrinth isn't easy, because as one spirals in, so one spirals into death. At the centre of the labyrinth resides Cerridwen's cauldron, and this is the cauldron of transformation, knowledge and rebirth, but before rebirth and knowledge can be bestowed, there has to be a death. There's no shortcut, this process cannot be avoided, and although it may happen over many stages and on many levels, happen it must. As I am walking towards the centre, I see the various things I have laid down over time, but there is more. The cauldron represents the womb of the Mother, and I am going to be expelled from this womb, born into a new place, but before this happens, I have to let go, and let go especially of the past—even of that which I think I have learned."

—Andy, www.paganinsomerset.blogspot.com

# The Pagan Labyrinth: The Goddess at the Center

# The Labyrinth: A Spiritual Journey

# The Pagan Labyrinth: The Goddess at the Center

The pagan Celts loved the Goddess, and their mythology was filled with her symbols. The goddess Cerridwen kept her cauldron—a womb symbol—in the circular labyrinthine fortress of Caer Sidi, and the labyrinth that circles around Glastonbury Tor also has ancient connections to chalice and well. These are vessels of change and rebirth, and Cerridwen is sometimes known as the goddess of transformation.

> Whoever has a desire to keep life safe
> will have it taken away;
> but whoever gives up life,
> will find life.
> —Jesus (Matthew 16:25)

For the infant, birth is a kind of death,

the end of all she has known up until that point,

a terrifying journey through a dark tunnel to another world.

Each death we undergo in life,

including the last and ultimate death,

is the same: both grave and womb,

an end and a beginning.

There is no escape.

We must die if we want to be born.

—Jayne Silverberry

> You cannot hope to find your way through the labyrinth
> unless you are willing to accept loss along the way.
> —William Bellford

Centuries before the Celts told their stories of Cerridwen and Caer Sidi, even before the Minoans living on the island of Crete recounted tales of Ariadne and the labyrinth, the ancient Sumerians had their own stories of Inanna, Queen of Heaven and Earth, who traveled into the underworld after the death of someone she loved. Inanna went through seven gates, and at each one, she shed an item of clothing or a piece of jewelry, until at last, by the time she reached the center of the underworld, she was naked—and then she was struck dead.

Inanna's body hung on a hook for three days (three is always a significant spiritual number!) before she came back to life. She escaped the underworld, and eventually, her husband took her place in the underworld for half the year, while her sister stood in for her for the rest of the year. When Inanna and her husband were reunited, the entire world flourishes—and when they were separated (just as in the Greek story of Persephone and Demeter), the Earth lay cold and barren. This ancient of story of death, resurrection, and renewal has been told in many ways in many places at many times, and ultimately, it is the story each of our lives tells.

## The Pagan Labyrinth: The Goddess at the Center

Like a seed growing into a tree, life unfolds stage by stage.

Triumphant ascent, collapse, crises, failures,

and new beginnings strew the way.

It is the path trodden by [all humans],

following its labyrinthine windings

from birth to death in hope and longing.

It is hedged about with struggle and suffering,

joy and sorrow, guilt and error,

and nowhere is there security from catastrophe.

Only if [we] tread the path bravely and fling [ourselves] into life,

fearing no struggle and no exertion

and fighting shy of no experience, will [we] mature.

—Jolanda Jacobi

# The Labyrinth: A Spiritual Journey

The Hopi people also connect the feminine with the labyrinth. The labyrinth shape, known both as the Mother and the Child and as the Emergence symbol, speaks of spiritual rebirth from one world to the next. Its shape is echoed in the kiva, the ceremonial circle structure with the sipapu in the center, the umbilical cord that leads to the underworld.

The seed that is to grow must lose itself as seed;
And they that creep may graduate through chrysalis to wings.
Will you then, O mortal, cling to husks
which falsely seem to you the self?
—Wu Ming Fu


Only the person who is born anew
will experience the reign of God.
—Jesus (John 3:3)

## The Pagan Labyrinth: The Goddess at the Center

These common themes of birth and rebirth, transformation and journeying echo through the mythology of cultures around the world. The labyrinth and the stories humans have told about it are archetypes, in the Jungian sense of the world, recurring patterns of human meaning we all understand at some level, no matter whether we are male or female. In our hearts, we all have both an intrepid hero and the hidden creative power to bring forth new life. If God is big enough to encompass both masculine and feminine, then surely we who are made in the Creator's image are the same—and we can recognize both Theseus and the Ariadne in ourselves. By the same token, when we reach the center of the labyrinth, we may have to face a monster—but we will also encounter the Divine.

> The creator of the world did not fashion
> these things directly from himself
> but copied them from archetypes outside himself.
> —Carl Jung

At one level, Christianity may have rejected these archetypes, but at a still deeper level, Christianity also embodied them. Just as the story of the fertility god (the god of grape and wheat) who died to bring new life to the world helped believers make sense of the Gospel, so the pagan labyrinth ultimately gave greater depth to Christian symbolism.

> By becoming fact it does not cease to
> be myth: that is the miracle.
> I suspect that [people] have sometimes
> derived more spiritual sustenance
> from myths they did not believe than from
> the religion they professed.
> To be truly Christian we must both assent to the historical fact
> and also receive the myth (fact though it has become)
> with the same imaginative embrace which we accord to all myths.
> The one is hardly more necessary than the other is.
>
> —C. S. Lewis

# The Pagan Labyrinth: The Goddess at the Center

# III
# The Medieval Labyrinth: The Christian Pilgrimage

## The Labyrinth: A Spiritual Journey

Starting in the eleventh century in Europe, labyrinths became a part of Christian worship. They were built into the floors of great cathedrals; smaller ones were sometimes posted on the walls outside the churches, to be traced with fingers until their ridges were nearly worn away. The most famous floor labyrinth is the one in the great cathedral of Chartres, a path of seven circles, cruciform in shape, which leads to a six-petaled rose—a symbol of Divine love—at its center. Other labyrinths were built in the cathedrals of Sens, Poitiers, Bayeaux, Amiens, and Rheims in France, and in Lucca and San Maria di Trastavera in Rome.

> Thou, Lord God, art my whole love and my desire!
> Thou art all mine and I all Thine!
> Spread my heart into Thy love that I may
> know how sweet it is to serve Thee,
> and to be as though I were entirely melted into Thy love.
> —Thomas á Kempis (medieval mystic)

# The Medieval Labyrinth: The Christian Pilgrimage

> Dear friends, I entreat you as pilgrims and sojourners
> not to indulge the cravings of your lower natures:
> for all such cravings wage war upon the soul.
>
> —1 Peter 2:11

Medieval Christians took seriously and literally the call in scripture to be pilgrims—to go on spiritual journeys through time and place. The Holy Land was the ultimate goal for these travelers, but of course not everyone could attempt such an expensive and lengthy trip. Instead, spiritual wayfarers might make less challenging pilgrimages to sites in Europe.

In many cases, the end of their journey was a labyrinth laid in the floor of the nave of one of the great Gothic cathedrals. Walking the labyrinth was the final leg of their pilgrimage, and reaching its center was a symbolic arrival at the Holy City. The labyrinth was sometimes referred to as the "Road to Jerusalem."

## The Medieval Labyrinth: The Christian Pilgrimage

For medieval followers of Christ, the labyrinth symbolized the human search for God. In the course of the labyrinth, sometimes the walker is close to God, sometimes far away, but the road always leads toward the center.

Those who walked the labyrinth's path in these great cathedrals would have at the same time been confronted with the visual symbolism of the great rose windows above them. The stained glass echoed the labyrinth's circle, as well as its focus on finding Christ at the center of life's turning wheel.

> The nature of God is a circle
> of which the center is everywhere
> and the circumference is nowhere.
> — Empedocles, fifth century BCE

# The Labyrinth: A Spiritual Journey

## The Medieval Labyrinth: The Christian Pilgrimage

The medieval mind reveled in symbolism. In a world where reading and writing were still skills reserved only for an elite few, visual symbols were the means for communicating spiritual instruction. Labyrinths and windows, the very architectural structure of the cathedral, were intended to teach the soul.

This meant that the Gospel was absorbed through the senses. The person who walked a labyrinth while gazing at the intricate jeweled circle of a stained-glass window took in spiritual truth wordlessly, sensually, in a far different way from what we are accustomed to today, with our dependence on the intellect and the written word.

> To further, then, the attainment of our due
> measure of becoming like God,
> the loving Source of all mysteries, . . .
> depicted in material images . . .
> so that we might be guided through the
> sensible to the intelligible,
> and from sacred symbols to the Primal Source.
> —Pseudo-Dionysius, fifth-sixth century

Medieval theologians were steeped in the thinking of great mystics like Dionysius the Areopagite (known better today as Pseudo-Dionysius, since his true identity is unknown). Dionysius wrote of the importance of symbols in the human journey to God; he believed spiritual truth is revealed through a great Celestial Hierarchy, circles within circles: many paths, many facets, all communicating a single Light.

> Every good and true thing is given to us from heaven,
> coming from the Father of lights.
>
> —James 1:17

## The Medieval Labyrinth: The Christian Pilgrimage

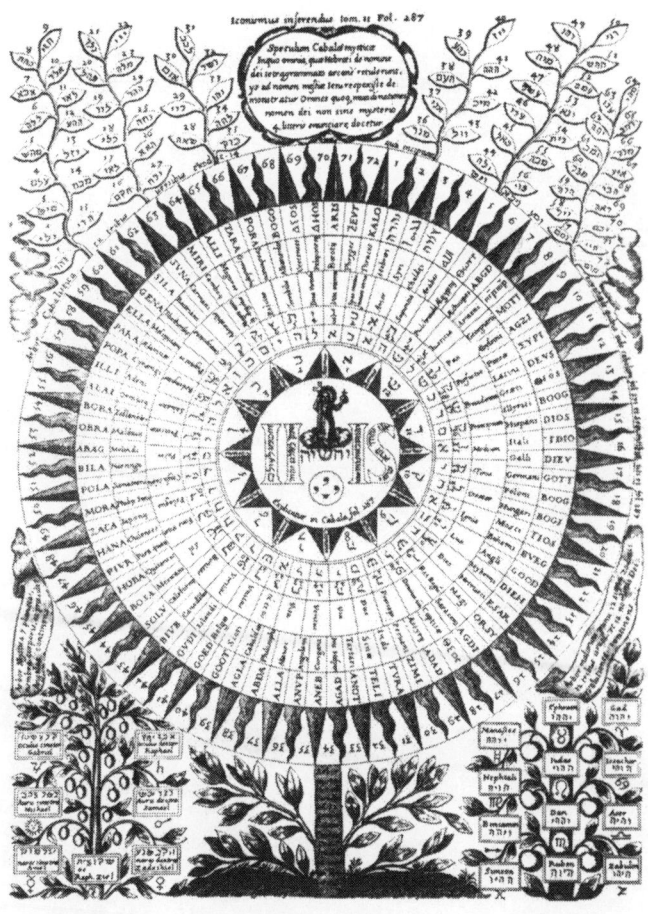

Moreover, every divine procession of radiance from the Father,
while constantly bounteously flowing to us,
fills us anew as though with a unifying power,
by recalling us to things above, and leading us to the unity
of the Shepherding Father and to the Divine One.
For from Him and into Him are all things,
as is written in the holy Word.
Calling then upon Jesus, the Light of
the Father, the Real and True,
"Which lights every man that comes into the world,
by whom we have access to the Father," the Origin of Light,
let us raise our thought, according to our power,
to the illumination of the most sacred doctrines . . .
revealed to us in symbols for our upliftment:
and admitting through the spiritual and
unwavering eyes of the mind

## The Medieval Labyrinth: The Christian Pilgrimage

the original and super-original gift of Light of
the Father who is the Source of Divinity,
which shows to us images of the all-blessed
Hierarchies of the Angels in figurative symbols,
let us through them again strive upwards toward Its primal ray.
For this Light can never be deprived of Its own intrinsic unity,
and although in goodness It becomes manyness
and proceeds into manifestation
for the uplifting of those creatures governed by Its providence,
yet It abides eternally within Itself in changeless sameness,
firmly established in Its own unity, and elevates to Itself,
according to their capacity, those who turn towards It,
uniting them in accordance with Its own unity.

—Pseudo-Dionysius

The circle of the Zodiac, the circle of the year (known in medieval terms as the "Labor of the Months"), the circles of the heavens were all portrayed in the great rose windows that lit the labyrinths. In the inmost circle, Christ would be seated, often with Mary, uniting the masculine and feminine into a single concept of the Divine One who rules all of life's circles. By meditating on these images, the medieval believer became joined with God.

> For each of those who is allotted a place in the Divine Order
> finds perfection in being uplifted,
> according to the capacity of each,
> toward the Divine Likeness; and what is still more divine,
> each becomes, as the Scriptures say, a fellow-worker with God,
> and shows forth the Divine Activity revealed
> as far as possible in each one.
> —Pseudo-Dionysius

## The Medieval Labyrinth: The Christian Pilgrimage

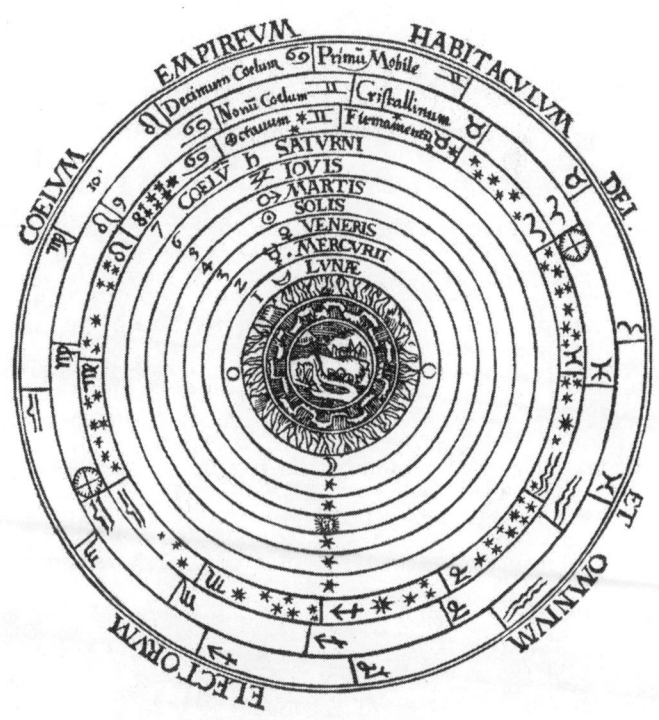

Many of us are accustomed today to think of worship as a solemn affair; we picture the medieval saints shuffling quietly around the labyrinth in a silent cathedral. Although these moments of subdued meditation likely did occur, labyrinths were also sites for a joyous game. Imagine this scene from the fifteenth century: on Easter Sunday, early in the afternoon, the canons and chaplains of the cathedral gather in the nave and form a circle around the labyrinth, while the congregation look on. As the men begin to move in the stately pattern of a ring-dance, they chant, "Vicitimae paschali laudes" (Praises to the Easter Victim). Meanwhile, the Dean of the cathedral stands in the center of the labyrinth and tosses a large leather ball to the dancers, who then lob it back to him. Before long, laughter and cheers would have rung through the cathedral!

> Rejoice in the Lord always; again I will say, rejoice!
> —Philippians 4:4

Unfortunately, later generations outlawed this childlike game of worship, and religion became a far stuffier thing. Many of the great labyrinths were destroyed, while the others lay ignored for centuries.

Then, in the twentieth century, human culture traveled back again on its journey toward God, arriving with a new perspective at an earlier path—and spiritual seekers once more turned to labyrinths for inspiration.

> The old order changeth, yielding place to new,
> And God fulfills himself in many ways,
> Lest one good custom should corrupt the world.
> —Alfred Lord Tennyson

# IV
# The Modern Labyrinth:
# A Threefold Journey

# The Labyrinth: A Spiritual Journey

> The longest journey
> Is the journey inwards.
> —Dag Hammarskjold

In the twentieth century, psychologists like Carl Jung drew new attention to the labyrinth as an archetypal symbol of the individuation process: the slow and twisty path toward the integration of the self, resolving layer after layer of psychological conflict to become whole. The goal of this journey is to let go of our old ways of being and thinking, so that we can reach the center, the Self, that which is the core of our identity—and there we will be renewed. But this is only half the journey. Once we reach the inner center with its treasure, we must then find our way out of the labyrinth and back to the outer world, forever transformed.

## The Modern Labyrinth: A Threefold Journey

This inward and outward expedition with its threefold steps of release, renew, return will be repeated over and over in our lives. And each time, we will come closer to the wholeness for which we were created.

> The labyrinth is also a symbol of integration, individuation,
> of the concentration of all essential layers,
> aspects, and levels of meaning of a human existence.
> It symbolizes, among other things, the process of maturation
> from a one-dimensional person ... into
> a rounded-out personality,
> composed in itself, which has found its center.
> —Hermann Kern

The first stage of the labyrinth's journey—release—asks that we let go of our demands on the universe. We give up our images of what life "ought" to be; we cease to insist on our own way. This perspective is contrary to other modern teachings that say we should fix our minds on the positive things we want and thereby attract those things to us. Release asks us to let all that go. The process is seldom easy; instead, this part of the journey is dark and painful. We must join Christ in the Garden of Gethsemane, when he prayed, "Not my will but Yours."

> We must be willing to get rid of the life we've planned,
> so as to have the life that is waiting for us.
> The old skin has to be shed before the new one can come.
> —Joseph Campbell

> The creative process is a process of surrender, not control.
> —Julia Cameron

And yet this seemingly negative perspective is also an affirmation of reality. By letting go of our fantasies and images, we say yes to what is. Once we have done that, creative work can be done both by us and through us. As we allow ourselves to be changed, we will change the world.

The road may be long and dreary—but ultimately it leads to new life and freedom. At the center of the labyrinth, after we have released all that held us back, we shall be renewed.

> Creative experience foreshadows a new Heaven and a new Earth.
> —Nikolai Berdyaev

# The Labyrinth: A Spiritual Journey

Each man's life is a labyrinth
at the centre of which lies his own death,
and even after death it may be
that he passes through a final maze
before it is all ended for him.
Within the great maze of a man's life are many smaller ones,
each seemingly complete in itself,
and in passing through each one he dies in part,
for in each he leaves behind him a part of his life
and it lies dead behind him.
It is a paradox of the labyrinth that the centre
appears to be the way to freedom.
—Michael Ayrton

> I want to be as though new-born, knowing
> nothing, absolutely nothing.
> —Paul Klee

To be renewed means to be made new, to be born again. We're familiar with the phrase "born again" as a religious term, but we seldom think about what it would mean literally. A newborn child has no preconceived notions about what the world should be like. She approaches life with a totally open mind, without judgment or prejudice. She does not compare herself to others; she simply *is*. She is open to possibility, to surprise, to new growth. This is equivalent to the "beginner's mind" recommended by Zen teachers: an attitude of openness and innocence.

Without a new birth

no one is able to see the kingdom of God.

—Jesus (John 3:3)


We think of things in a straight line: birth-life-death.

That's not really how it works.

You take those ends and you bend it into a circle

so it's birth-life-death-REbirth.

—Will Smith


Be renewed in the spirit of your mind

and put on the new self.

—Ephesians 4:23–24

When we are in this state of newness, emptied of all we once were, we can at last find ourselves. Paradoxically, we must lose ourselves in order to find ourselves. We must let our egos die, so that our true selves can be born. And when we find our true selves, we will also find God.

> Have this mind in you, which was also in Christ Jesus:
> who, existing in the form of God,
> counted not the being on an equality with
> God a thing to be grasped,
> but emptied himself..., becoming obedient even unto death.
> —Philippians 2:5–8

God is always the first person, the I, ever standing before you.

Because you give precedence to worldly things,

God appears to have receded to the background.

If you give up all else and seek him alone,

he alone will remain as the "I," the Self. . . .

Of all the definitions of God,

none is indeed so well put as the Biblical statement

"I am that I am" in Exodus 3. . . .

The absolute being is what is.

It is the Self. It is God.

Knowing the Self, God is known.

—Sri Ramana Maharshi

## The Modern Labyrinth: A Threefold Journey

Once we reach the center of the labyrinth and experience the renewal we find there, we must return to the outer world. This is life's constant cycle: we first turn inward in order to know ourselves and God—and then we turn once more to the outer world. The creative work of life requires this back-and-forth between a quiet introspection of the spirit and an active involvement in external reality.

> Personal transformation can and does have global effects.
> As we go, so goes the world, for the world is us.
> The revolution that will save the world
> is ultimately a personal one.
> —Marianne Williamson

> We think of time as a straight line.
>
> But it is a circle.
>
> Never fear when you think you have reached the end.
>
> Continue on into the next phase.
>
> There is no end.
>
> —Mary Coogan

The labyrinth, that ancient myth with its connections to both monsters and goddesses, remains a living archetype: in Jungian terms, a universal pattern that shapes human thought, that recurs again and again, around the world, across the centuries. Like a mathematical fractal that repeats its pattern again and again, in large and small ways, the labyrinth circles through human thought.

The Power of the World always works in circles,

and everything and everything tries to be round.

… Everything the power of the world does is done in a circle.

The sky is round and I have heard that the earth is round like a ball

and so are all the stars. The wind, in its greatest power, whirls.

Birds make their nests in circles, for theirs

is the same religion as ours.

The sun comes forth and goes down again in a circle. The moon

does the same and both are round. Even the seasons form a great

circle in their changing and always come

back again to where they were.

The life of a man is a circle from childhood to childhood, and so it is

in everything where power moves. Our teepees were round like the

nests of birds, and these were always set

in a circle, the nation's hoop,

a nest of many nests, where the Great Spirit

meant for us to hatch our children.

—Black Elk, Holy Man of the Oglala Sioux, nineteenth century

The labyrinth's circle with its twists and turns remains a meaningful symbol of ultimate reality. At the same time, it is a powerful tool for jumpstarting our spiritual awareness. And yet it is only a tool, the symbol rather than the thing itself. Ultimately, as you walk the labyrinth, remember: the labyrinth is always open to the sky. A greater, fuller reality lies beyond.

You may chant and meditate, . . .

and dwell at sacred shrines of pilgrimage;

. . . but without the True One, what is the use of it all?

—Sri Guru Granth Sahib

# The Modern Labyrinth: A Threefold Journey

In my end is my beginning.
—Mary, Queen of Scots

## CHECK OUT THESE OTHER TITLES FROM
# ANAMCHARA BOOKS
### WWW.ANAMCHARABOOKS.COM

**The Dragon Within Your Heart**
Price: $12.95 Paperback
5 x 7 inches
100 pages
ISBN: 978-1-937211-14-1

*We all have [a dragon inside us], in one form or another.
. . . both the wild nature of ourselves
and our conscience . . . [and]
our unconscious,
the place from which our dreams arise.
—Dennis Quaid*

None of us has ever seen a dragon in the external world—and yet all of us would recognize one if we did.

But dragons don't exist "out there." They live inside us, within our hearts as much as our imagination. They tell us something about our own nature. They remind us that despite our scales and gnarled claws, our vanity and greed, we have wings strong enough to lift us out of our dark caverns.

Dragons bring out the best in us; they call to us with God's voice.

**Water from an Ancient Well:
Celtic Spirituality for Modern Life**
Price: $24.95 Paperback
5.25 x 8 inches
352 pages
ISBN: 978-1-933630-98-4

**In story, scripture, reflection, and prayer,
taste the living water that refreshed the ancient Celts.**

"This book will invite you to a new way of seeing."
—Ray Simpson, author of *Soul Friendship* and *Celtic Light*

Discover the world of the ancient Celtic Christians—and find practical insights for living in the twenty-first century. Using storytelling, careful research, and personal experience, the author invites you to get to know Brendan and Brigid, Columba and Patrick, as well as Myrddin (better known as Merlin) and other lesser-known figures from the great pageant of Celtic history. These stories both entertain and inspire; rooted in legend and history, they offer us here-and-now hope and insight.

**Hazelnuts of Grace:
Selections from Julian of Norwich**
Price: $12.95 Paperback
5 x 7 inches
152 pages
ISBN: 978-1-937211-10-3

*The Spirit showed me a tiny thing the size of a hazelnut,
as round as a ball and so small I could hold it in the palm of my hand.
I . . . wondered, "What is this?" The answer came to me:
"This is everything that has been made. This is all Creation."
It was so small that I marveled it could endure;
such a tiny thing seemed likely to simply fall into nothingness.
Again the answer came to my thoughts:
"It lasts, and it will always last, because God loves it."*

These selections taken from *All Shall Be Well*, Anamchara Books' modern-language version of the complete revelation of Julian of Norwich, are arranged thematically, bite-size thoughts to be read slowly, one at a time. This is the sort of book that's meant to be picked up for five minutes and put down again . . . while a kernel of truth lingers in your mind, transforming your thoughts. Each short selection contains within it Julian's amazing message:

**all shall be well**
*because God's love sustains our world.*

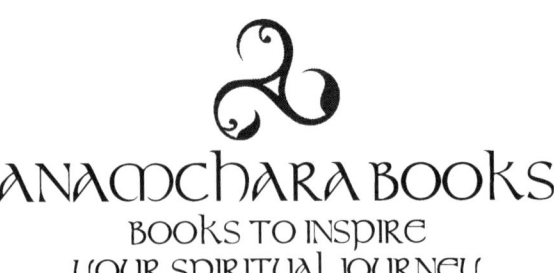

# ANAMCHARA BOOKS
## BOOKS TO INSPIRE
## YOUR SPIRITUAL JOURNEY

In Celtic Christianity, an *anamchara* is a soul friend, a companion and mentor (often across the miles and the years) on the spiritual journey. Soul friendship entails a commitment to both accept and challenge, to reach across all divisions in a search for the wisdom and truth at the heart of our lives.

At Anamchara Books, we are committed to creating a community of soul friends by publishing books that lead us into deeper relationships with God, the Earth, and each other. These books connect us with the great mystics of the past, as well as with more modern spiritual thinkers. They are designed to build bridges, shaping an inclusive spirituality where we all can grow.

You can order our books at **www.AnamcharaBooks.com**. Check out our site to read opinions and perspectives from our editorial staff on our Soul Friends blog. You can also submit your own blog posts by emailing **info@AnamcharaBooks.com** with "Blog Entry for Soul Friends" in the subject line. To find out more about Anamchara Books and connect with others on their own spiritual journeys, visit **www.AnamcharaBooks.com** today.

## ANAMCHARA BOOKS
220 Front Street
Vestal, New York 13850
(607) 785-1578
*www.AnamcharaBooks.com*

Made in the USA
Charleston, SC
09 July 2011